Dedication Page

This book is dedicated to my little brother Zaim, He helped me a lot, he is the best brother ever to help me, and he helped me make the lemonade and we sold the lemonade together' - Sareem Ahsan
(7 years old)

On a warm summer morning of August 2023, Sareem woke up with an idea buzzing in his mind. As he finished his breakfast, he approached his father in the living room with excitement sparkling in his eyes.

His father looked up from his black laptop and smiled.
"That's a great idea, Sareem. But every business needs a solid plan.
Why don't you create a business plan first, and then
I'll help with your initial investment?"

What will make my lemonade stand different?

Sareem grabbed his iPad and dashed to his room. He spent hours brainstorming, typing furiously, and sketching out his ideas.

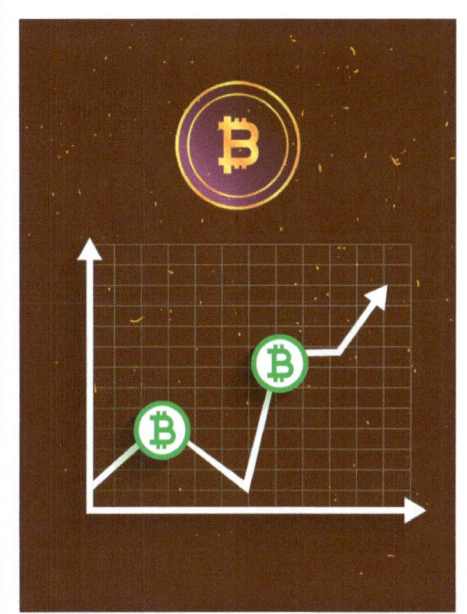

As he listed flavors and pricing, his excitement grew. By the time he finished, he had a detailed plan: a menu, pricing, and even a special touch to stand out.

Sareem comes to the living room to ask his dad for help and his dad helped him create and brainstorm his plan together, adding expenses and forecasting profits, budgeting a plan with Sareem.

The next day, Sareem presented his completed plan to his father.

I've thought of everything!" he said proudly.
His father read through the plan, nodding. "This is impressive, Sareem.
Let's go shopping for supplies this weekend and make this happen."
Overjoyed, Sareem started listing all the items he would need for
his stand: lemons, sugar, a dispenser, and even decorations.

The weekend arrived, and Sareem and his father headed to the store. Sareem's mother helped carefully pick out the freshest lemons and bright red pomegranates for his special drinks.

On the day of his first event,
Sareem set up his lemonade stand with care.

He stood proudly behind his table with his little brother
Zaim right next to him, waiting for his first customer.

The first customer, his Grandma that he calls 'DaDa' visited for some of his special lemonade. Sareem smiled as he scooped fresh pomegranate seeds into her drink.

Wow, this looks delicious!" she said, sipping her lemonade.
Word spread quickly, and soon Sareem's stand was crowded.

By the end of the day, Sareem was thrilled
to see his jar filled with money.
He counted his earnings: $183!

The next event was a bit quieter. Sareem worried he wouldn't make many sales until a boy his age approached. "I really want lemonade, but I don't have any money," the boy said.

Sareem had an idea. "How about you help me bring customers, and I'll pay you $1 for every lemonade sold?

The boy darted into the crowd, enthusiastically waving the menu and talking to anyone who would listen. "Have you tried Sareem's lemonade? It's the best here!" he called out.

Customers began trickling in, and Sareem stayed busy making drinks. By the end of the day, the boy had earned his own lemonade and a few extra dollars. Sareem counted his earnings: $206. He couldn't believe it!

For his third event, Sareem decided to try something new.
"I'll raise the price a little," he thought.
"And I'll offer a mix-and-match deal for customers who want more!"
He updated his sign to read:
1 Lemonade for $3 – 2 for $5!

LEMONADE

Special
1 Lemonade
for $3
–
2 for $5

The new pricing worked like magic. Customers loved the options, and Sareem made $202 that day.

With each event, Sareem grew more confident.
On his 4th event in December 2024, He started
experimenting with additional items like halal gummies for kids.
"These will give customers more choices," he reasoned.

The extra items helped boost his sales. By the end of the fourth event, Sareem had made $261, bringing his total earnings to $852.

Sareem's Lemonade Stand

That night, Sareem sat at the dining table with his earnings spread out in front of him.
"I finally did it!" he said, counting the bills again.
His father looked at him proudly.
"You've worked so hard, Sareem.
Are you ready to buy your PS5 PRO?"

"Yes!" Sareem exclaimed, grinning from ear to ear.

At the electronics store, Sareem handed over his hard-earned money to the cashier.
"Here's your PS5 PRO," the cashier said, handing him the box.

Sareem held it tightly, beaming with pride.
"This is the best reward for my hard work," he thought.

Although he had achieved his goal,
Sareem took time to reflect on the challenges he faced.

"Sometimes I ran out of supplies or didn't get paid on time," he recalled. "But I learned how to adapt and keep going." Every setback had taught him a valuable lesson.

One of the biggest lessons he learned was about engaging with customers.
"Standing in front of the stand and making eye contact really helped,"
Sareem noted. "It's important to connect with people."

He also realized the importance of keeping things organized and planning ahead.

Sareem's hard work didn't just earn him a PS5 PRO

It also gave him valuable skills for the future.

"I learned how to manage money, solve problems, and think creatively," he said.

These were lessons he would carry with him for life.

Sareem's story inspired others.
At school, his friends asked him about the lemonade stand.
"How did you do it?" they asked.
"I started with a plan," Sareem explained.
"And I never gave up, even when things got tough."

Work Smart,
Play Hard.

Write your Life

Sareem also realized the importance of rewarding himself.
"Hard work deserves celebration," he thought,
remembering how happy he felt buying his PS5 PRO.

He encouraged others to set goals and reward themselves too.

As summer ended, Sareem began thinking about new ideas

"Maybe a popcorn and cotton candy stand in the winter
or a community event fundraiser!"
He also has an idea of writing a book for his
lemonade stand journey.
The possibilities seemed endless.

Through his journey, Sareem realized that being an entrepreneur was about more than just making money.

"It's about connecting with people, solving problems, and bringing joy," he said.

And that was something he wanted to keep doing.

SAREEM'S LEMONADE

Original Lemonade $1
Pomegranate Lemonade $1

SPECIAL 3 FOR $5 Lemonade

Juice

Water $1
$1

Lemonade Plan
Friday, August 25, 2023   8:56 AM

What do I need?
- Table - rent $25-$50
- Cups - $20 for 200
- Table cloth $1.50
- Picture frame for menu $1.50
- 2 gallon glass dispenser $40
- Menu printed - Free

One time expense total: $88

Lemonade Cost
24 lemonades
2 gallon water

Estimate cost $100

Estimated return on 200 cups $400

Profit $300

Lemonade event at

Table cost: $65
Dispenser cost: $44

Menu add on:
Water & juice box

True expense was $220

We must sell $220 to break even

Bring 100 ones as change
100 in 10s & 5s
Take Venmo

50 cups lemonade = $100
50 cups pomegranate = $150

Water 35 packs = $35
Fruit barrel = $40

If we sell out we make $325

Key Takeaways

1.   Create a Business Plan: Always make a comprehensive business plan before starting any venture. This plan should outline your goals, strategies, and potential challenges.

2.   Budget and Forecast Realistically: Ensure your budget and financial forecasts are aligned with realistic expectations. Overestimating can lead to disappointment, while underestimating can limit growth.

3.   Expect Shrinkage: Understand that theft and shrinkage are normal in any business. Plan for these losses to mitigate their impact.

4.   Engage with Customers: In sales, it's important to stand in front of your stand, make eye contact with every potential customer, and always be on an equal level. If your customers are standing, you should stand too. Show respect and build a connection.

5.   Reward Yourself: Always have a reward at the end to appreciate your hard work. It's essential to celebrate your achievements and stay motivated.

Lesson Learned: The Importance of Planning and Budgeting

Lesson Learned: Learning from Challenges Like Theft and Shrinkage

Lesson Learned: Reward Yourself

Work Smart,
Play Hard.

Write your Life

Sareem's lemonade stand journey was just the beginning. With his entrepreneurial spirit and determination, there was no limit to what he could achieve.
And as he played on his PS5 PRO that evening, he smiled, knowing that hard work and creativity could turn dreams into reality.

Lemonade Plan

Friday, August 25, 2023   8:56 AM

What do I need?

- Table - rent $25-$50
- Cups - $20 for 200
- Table cloth $1.50
- Picture frame for menu $1.50
- 2 gallon glass dispenser $40
- Menu printed - Free

One time expense total: $88

Lemonade Cost

24 lemonades
2 gallon water

Estimate cost $100

Estimated return on 200 cups $400

Profit $300

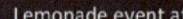

Lemonade event at [redacted]

Table cost: $65
Dispenser cost: $44

Menu add on:
Water & juice box

Bring 100 ones as change
100 in 10s & 5s
Take Venmo

True expense was $220

We must sell $220 to break even

50 cups lemonade = $100
50 cups pomegranate = $150

Water 35 packs = $35
Fruit barrel = $40

If we sell out we make $325

Author

With Contributions from
Sameul Ahsan

Sareem is a young entrepreneur with big dreams. Born in Worcester, MA, he planned and launched his first lemonade stand at just 6 years old. By the age of 7, he achieved his goal of earning enough to purchase a PS5 Pro by the end of 2024. Sareem aspires to grow his entrepreneurial journey by exploring new ventures, scaling his business, and leading others to drive future projects to success.

As a father, Sameul Ahsan is deeply committed to financial literacy, recognizing that these essential skills are often overlooked in traditional education. He ensures that Sareem and Zaim actively engage in budgeting, investing, and entrepreneurship, empowering them to build a strong foundation for their future.

With over 12 years of leadership experience, Sameul has managed teams across New England and, as a Director, has driven profitability for retail locations. His passion for real estate began at 23 with his first multifamily investment, leading to a successful short-term rental business.

Special Thanks

To Sareem's grandmother, Sabina Chowdhury (lovingly called 'DaDa'), for her unwavering support and for always being his first and most loyal customer.
And to his mother, Maliha Mahi, whose tireless dedication, love, and hard work made this journey possible. From late nights peeling pomegranates to ensuring every detail was just right, she was the heart behind Sareem's success, always guiding and supporting him every step of the way.

What happens when a young boy has a big idea?
He turns it into a business!

Join Sareem on an exciting journey filled with hard work, creativity, and determination—all beginning with a simple lemonade stand. From crafting a business plan to making his first sale, Sareem discovers valuable lessons about money, customers, and perseverance.
Based on a true story, Sareem's Lemonade Stand encourages kids everywhere to dream big, take action, and embark on their own exciting adventures!

"An idea brought to life can turn into something amazing!"

Author: Sareem Ahsan
Illustrator: Ibaad Malik
With contributions from: Sameul Ahsan

$14.99
ISBN 979-8-9925597-0-5
51499>

9 798992 559705

www.ingramcontent.com/pod-product-compliance
Lightning Source LLC
Chambersburg PA
CBHW041552120626

46551CB00002B/185